curiouşabout

GUINEA PIGS

BY ALISSA THIELGES

AMICUS

What are you

A guinea pig cage should include safe places for your pet to hide.

DID YOU KNOW?
Guinea pigs live five to seven years.

Can I keep more than one guinea pig at a time?

Two guinea pigs are better than one.

Yes! Guinea pigs are very **social**. They are happiest when around others. Two guinea pigs can keep each other company. They may **bond** and play. Just remember, they will need a lot of space. Their cage should be twice as big.

ABYSSINIAN

PERUVIAN

TEDDY

AMERICAN

TEXEL

Can I let my guinea pig run around my room?

Yes. His main home should be a cage. But he can come out to play. Keep an eye on him. You don't want him to get lost. Guinea pigs also pee and poop anywhere. You may have to clean up a stinky surprise. A small space with a towel works best.

Keep an eye on your guinea pig when you let him out!

What do pet guinea pigs eat?

Guinea pigs are **herbivores**. They chew on hay all day. It wears down their teeth, which are always growing. Guinea pigs also need veggies and fruits. These foods give them vitamin C.

Leafy greens are healthy snacks for a guinea pig.

GUINEA PIG FOOD

Big Meal:
hay, pellets

Small Treats:
apples, carrots

Snacks:
kale or other
leafy vegetables

Why does my guinea pig jump up and down?

A guinea pig may jump for joy when it's happy.

She is excited! This is called popcorning. She's having fun and loving playtime. Guinea pigs do this a lot with each other. They chase and jump. They may twist in the air and squeak. It's a jump for joy!

DID YOU KNOW?
Young guinea pigs popcorn more often than adults.

Do guinea pigs ever sleep?

A guinea pig takes short naps.

Yes, but only in short bursts. Guinea pigs are very active. They're awake about 20 hours each day. They nap a few minutes at a time. Sometimes, they don't even close their eyes!

Yuck. My guinea pig eats his poop! Why?

A guinea pig w
poop anywher

This is healthy! But don't worry, it's not true poop. It is **caecotroph** (SEE-ko-trof). It is soft. It still has food that wasn't digested all the way. Your pet gulps it down for nutrients. It helps his gut stay healthy. His other poop is dark and hard. It looks like pellets. He won't eat this. It can be thrown away.

DID YOU KNOW?
If a guinea pig is licking its butt, it may be eating its poop.

Do guinea pigs oink?

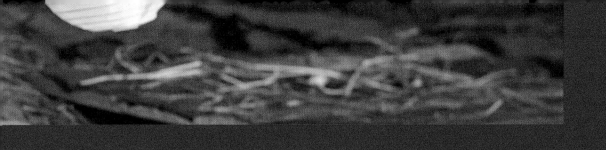

Sort of. Guinea pigs are **rodents**, not pigs. But their squeal sounds like a high-pitched oink. That's how they got their name. The noise is called wheeking. It means your pet is excited! She sees food. Or she may want to be petted.

Guinea pigs may wheek when it's time to eat.

DID YOU KNOW?
Guinea pigs are also called cavies. They came from South America.

Why do guinea pigs purr?

Purring can mean different things. Is your pet calm and relaxed? He is happy. He might purr when petted. Is he tense? He may be annoyed. This purr will have a higher **pitch**. A short purr can signal fear. That guinea pig will be very still.

It can be hard to tell how a guinea pig is feeling.

ASK MORE QUESTIONS

How did guinea pigs become pets?

Why do guinea pigs sleep with their eyes open?

Try a BIG QUESTION: Why do people keep pets?

SEARCH FOR ANSWERS

Search the library catalog or the Internet.
A librarian, teacher, or parent can help you.

Using Keywords
Find the looking glass.

Keywords are the most important words in your question.

?

If you want to know about:

- when guinea pigs became pets, type: GUINEA PIG ORIGIN

- how to take care of a guinea pig, type: GUINEA PIG CARE

FIND GOOD SOURCES

Here are some good, safe sources you can use in your research. Your librarian can help you find more.

Books

Be a Hamster and Guinea Pig Expert by Gemma Barder, 2021.

Guinea Pigs by Christina Leaf, 2021.

Internet Sites

Guinea Pig Cages: Setup & Recommendations https://www.guineapighub.com/guinea-pig-cages/ Guinea Pig Hub is a popular blog for guinea pig care advice and tips.

Smithsonian's National Zoo—Guinea Pig https://nationalzoo.si.edu/animals/guinea-pig The Smithsonian is a national organization that researches wild animals.

Every effort has been made to ensure that these websites are appropriate for children. However, because of the nature of the Internet, it is impossible to guarantee that these sites will remain active indefinitely or that their contents will not be altered.

SHARE AND TAKE ACTION

Pet sit a friend's guinea pig.

Teach others about guinea pig behavior and sounds. Be a role model on how to care for these pets.

Volunteer at an animal shelter. They may have guinea pigs or other small pets you can help.

GLOSSARY

bond To form a close friendship or connection.

caecotroph A soft pellet made by a guinea pig's digestion that comes out of its butt and is eaten for nutrition.

herbivore An animal that only eats plants for energy.

pitch The highness or lowness of a sound.

rodent A mammal with large, sharp front teeth that never stop growing.

social Friendly and liking to be around people or other animals.

INDEX

About the Author

Alissa Thielges is a writer and editor in southern Minnesota who hopes to inspire kids to stay curious about their interests. She doesn't own any pets but would love to have a turtle and dog someday.